M

WHERE DOES GOD LIVE?

"A compelling and touching book—a delight
for parents and children both to read, and a
book like no other I know on a subject of
great import to millions of us!"
ROBERT COLES, M.D.
Author of *The Spiritual Life of Children*

"When a rabbi and a monsignor meet to
exchange stories and ideas about God, I am
sure that God listens. And so do many Jews
and many Christians."
ELIE WIESEL
Nobel Peace Laureate

"A delightful and timely book for children
and their parents. Its prayerful reading will
bring families and Churches closer together.
We need such efforts to achieve true peace.
I strongly recommend this fine book."
REV. THEODORE M. HESBURGH, C.S.C.
President Emeritus
University of Notre Dame

WHERE DOES GOD LIVE?

Rabbi Marc Gellman and
Monsignor Thomas Hartman

BALLANTINE BOOKS • NEW YORK

Sale of this book without a cover may be unauthorized. If this book is coverless, it may have been reported to the publisher as "unsold or destroyed" and neither the author nor the publisher may have received payment for it.

Copyright © 1991 by Marc Gellman and Thomas Hartman

All rights reserved under International and Pan-American Copyright Conventions. Published in the United States by Ballantine Books, a division of Random House, Inc., New York, and simultaneously in Canada by Random House of Canada Limited, Toronto.

No part of this publication may be reproduced, stored in a retrieval system, or transmitted in any form or by any means—electronic, mechanical, photocopy, recording, or any other—except for brief quotations, in printed reviews, without the prior permission of the publisher.

Library of Congress Catalog Card Number: 90-25458

ISBN 0-345-37795-8

This edition published by arrangement with Gleneida Publishing Group

Printed in Canada

First Ballantine Books Edition: September 1992
Fourth Printing: April 1993

For Larry Fraiberg,
who brought me to choices
informed by both the spirit and the mind . . .
                              Tom Hartman

For Ron Miller,
who brought me to common ground . . .
                              Marc Gellman

CONTENTS

CONTENTS

THANKS . . .

We would especially like to thank our editor, Ms. Patricia Kossmann, who was usually patient and always wise. She knew what to take out and what to leave in.

We would like to thank all those friends who read earlier versions of this book: Gail Belva, Tony Curto, Naami Kelman, Joanne Kroon, Marilyn Levy, Jeff Salkin, Stephanie Schulman, Alexei Simonov, Paul Stallsworth, Susan Stone, Gerry Twomey, and other friends who reminded us of forgotten important things just in the nick of time and each in his or her own way.

God bless them all!
Marc Gellman and Tom Hartman

FIRST THINGS FIRST . . .
FOR KIDS

One of us is a priest and one of us is a rabbi, and we wrote this book because we wanted to share our love of God and our love of people, who are made special like God. We are good friends, and one of the most important things we learned by being friends is something we know, but sometimes forget: we as Jews and Christians may have different holidays and different prayers, but we have the EXACT SAME God.

How wonderful it is that we have different holidays and different prayers, but how very wonderful it is that we have the same God, because it means that really we are more the same than we are different. Now, for some Christians, and for some Jews, who think we are more different than the same, this book may take a little getting used to. Some folks think that if we talk about how we are the same we will forget about how we are different, and we will forget how to do some of those special things which make us different. We don't think so. What we think is that we talk enough and know enough about how we are different, but we don't talk enough and know enough about how we are the same. And that is why we wrote this book.

This book might be good for you to read alone. It might be good for your parents to read to you. It might be good for your parents to read alone. What we hope is that as you are reading this book, you will also be talking with your parents about God. Believe us! Talking about God is much better than talking about homework and slightly better than talking about baseball.

We know that many times when you want to talk to your parents about God, they don't know what to say. That is another reason we wrote this book. We want to give your parents something to say when you ask them about God. The standard parent answer to God questions is "Go ask the priest!" or "Go ask the rabbi!" or "Go ask the minister!" depending, of course, on what religion you are. This is not a bad answer, because rabbis, ministers, and priests have good and wise things to teach you about God, but it is not a good enough answer. When

2

you ask your parents about God, you should hear what *they* believe about God—not what your minister, priest, or rabbi believes about God.

If you are always sent to your priest, minister, or rabbi to learn about God, you might think that to know anything about God, you have to be some kind of God expert. But knowing about God is not like knowing about plumbing (where you really do need to go to a plumbing expert or your house will leak!). You don't have to be a rabbi, priest, or minister to be an expert about God. Lots of people, maybe including your parents, are God experts, and lots of people can teach you about God. The people who are God experts (the people you want to learn from) are any people who have let God into their lives, and who are trying to do what God wants them to do in the world.

Priests and ministers and rabbis have wonderful and wise things to say about God, and it is very important to go to church or synagogue and pray together, and sing together, and study together about God. But it is also important that you talk about God in your home. God does not live just in your church or your synagogue. God also lives in your home. God should be a part of your life at home and at school, at work and at play. God should be important to all the parts of your life. Your life will be better and bigger, more loving and more helpful, if you take God with you when you leave church or

3

synagogue to go home. So, we hope this book gets you talking about God with your parents and with your friends, and not just with your priest or minister or rabbi.

We love children, and one thing we have learned is that almost all kids have the same questions about God. Christian children and Jewish children all wonder about God in pretty much the same exact way. So what we did was put together in this book the questions kids have asked us most about God, and then we tried to give answers to those questions.

But answering questions about God is not like answering questions about pizza. God is much harder to talk about and much harder to know about than pizza. With a pizza, you've got your basic crust, and your basic tomato sauce, and your basic cheese and your basic toppings and . . . that's a pizza. The reason we know so much about pizzas is that we see piz-zas, and eat pizzas, all the time. But God is different from a pizza. God is not like anything else in the world. God cannot be seen and God cannot be smelled. But God is as real as pizza—more real because (although you may find this hard to believe) there was a time before pizza, but *there never was a time before God*.

The answers to the questions about God in this book are only our answers. If you have dif-ferent answers to these questions that is just fine. As long as you are asking questions about

God you are on the right track and God will help you find the right answers.

If there are some other questions you have about God which we did not put in this book just write to us and we will try to put them in our next book. You can write to us at Ballantine Books, 201 East 50th Street, New York, NY 10022. We hope that this book will help you come closer to God, because God is already very close to you. Closer than you could ever, ever know.

God bless you!

Marc Gellman and Tom Hartman

FIRST THINGS FIRST . . .
FOR PARENTS

Parents usually don't know how to answer their children's questions about God, and Jewish and Christian children ask the same questions about God. These are the reasons we wrote this book. These are also the reasons we wrote this book together. We collected and answered the common questions asked by children about God. Each chapter is a question and an answer. What we hope is that these questions and answers will help you in talking to your child about God. The questions are not the only questions, and the answers are not dogma. They are just a way to begin.

One of us is a priest and one of us is a rabbi, and we believed that it would be both possible and wonderful to try to teach Jewish and

Christian children in the same way about the God we share. We did this in full understanding and respect for the differences that distinguish Judaism from Christianity. However, we believe that those differences do not alter or compromise the historical and theological fact that Jews and Christians share a common faith in a common God.

The questions in this book should be familiar to even very young children, but some of the answers may be a little difficult for them. They may need your help here and there to explain some of the concepts. We have simplified only the language—not the ideas—in this book. Older children should be able to handle it all with ease, but even in their case we encourage you to read the chapters along with them. Remember that the aim of the book is to help you and your child get started talking about God together.

Please don't be fearful. We understand just how difficult it is to answer a child's simple, direct, and innocent questions about God. Such questions are almost always unexpected. We understand that for many parents, Godtalk may seem awkward at first. But we believe that with patience and a few pointers you can, and you should, have wonderful conversations with your child about God.

Here are some things you can do:

1. *Let your child watch you do the religious things you do.*

The best way to explain God to children is without words. Letting them see you engaged in religious behavior will do more than a thousand books to stimulate questions and teach them that God is real in your life and ought to be real in theirs.

If they see you pray, they will want to know about prayer. If you just tell them about prayer, they may not care at all. If they see you reading the Bible, they will want to know what is in it. If you just tell them about the Bible, they may not care at all. If they see you observing holidays, they will want to know what they mean. If you just tell them about the holidays, they may not care at all. They learn to cook by watching you cook. They learn to read by watching you read. It is no different with God. They will learn about God by seeing how God is a part of your life.

2. *Tell your children what you believe, while making it clear to them that they must decide for themselves what they believe.*

This book follows the clear teachings of Judaism and of Christianity in stressing our freedom to choose to love God. God wants us to choose to let God into our lives, to choose to do what God wants us to do. Children must understand that you, their parents, have chosen to believe in God, and that you hope they will make the same choice, but a child must know that it is his or her right and responsibility to make this choice. You can and will teach them, but at some time God must become their God by an act of will and love and faith. In this way a belief in God is not being imposed on them but is being offered to them out of your love for God and your desire to follow God's commandments in your life.

3. *Don't be afraid to say "I don't know" when talking to your child about God.*

It is very important for children to try to understand something that cannot be completely understood. God is real but complex. The message that not all reality is easy to understand is an important message. It will lead to curiosity and further reflection rather than to frustration and confusion. Try to follow any statements of what you don't *know* with statements of what you *believe*. The truth of the matter is that when a child asks you about God, he or she is asking not only about God but also about you.

4. *Try to relate God to how we live, not just to what we believe.*

It is too easy for Godtalk to become abstract and irrelevant in our lives. God is not just some remote being living at the far edge of the universe. The God of Judaism and Christianity is a God who is in our world—immanent and loving, yet also commanding. Belief in God produces a change not just in our ideas about the world, but, more fundamentally, a change in the way we live in this world. God wants us to live in a certain way, not just think in a certain way, and so the connection between God and our moral lives must be clear and strong to children. God is the reason for the good things we do, and so what God wants us to do is a more religiously significant question than what God is.

5. *Don't give answers about God which are too simple.*

In this book we have tried to simplify the language, not the concepts. The issues engaged in this book are deep and ancient questions of philosophy and theology. They are not easy. They do not go away when we say a few words about them. Children deserve the right to chew on big, rich, complicated ideas. Children deserve an encounter with God which lets them peek into the depths of true mystery. Children deserve to be introduced to a God whose complex and infinite attributes will unfold before them, not in the span of a single bedtime story but over a lifetime of loving reflection, prayer, and religiously motivated action.

Finally, we hope that the book is useful to adults as well. The questions asked by children about God are, honestly, no different, except for their candor and simplicity, from the questions asked by adults. There is nothing to say that an adult cannot come to God the way a child comes to God.

If you don't believe in God, you can still talk meaningfully to your child about God (provided of course you have the inclination). If you do proceed from an atheistic or agnostic perspective (the latter is obviously much easier to work with), we beg you not to cut off your child's ability to believe. Explain to him or her that even though you may have doubts about whether God is real, God is still a living force in many people's lives and God could be that for them. You must know and your children must know that doubts about God can be a part of faith. It is only our indifference to God, our lack of concern for anything spiritual, that causes the death of faith, because such indifference quenches the fires of curiosity and spirituality which lead us to faith in God.

Beyond these ideas and suggestions, we really have only one other notion about whom this book is for. This book is for God. Every true word is surely due to God's help. Every false word is undoubtedly due to our stubbornness, impatience, or ignorance. For the former, we give thanks to God. For the latter, we ask forgiveness.

1

IS GOD REAL?
PART 1—NATURE

God is very good, very kind, very powerful, very smart, and very invisible. God is not like anything else. This makes it hard to know about God. We know about all things other than God by seeing them, hearing them, tasting them, touching them, or smelling them. We are used to knowing things that way. But we just can't see, smell, hear, taste, or touch God. This means that we can't use the ways we know about other things to know about God.

We know about God by seeing, hearing, touching, tasting, and smelling the things God has made. These things are things which only God could have made, and so when we see, hear, touch, taste, or smell these things we know that God is real even if we can't see, hear, touch, taste or smell God.

One thing only God could have made which shows us that God is real is good old Mother Nature. A lot of people feel close to God when they are out in nature: when they walk in a forest, or watch a pretty sunset, or see a high mountain or a waterfall. People who feel close to God when they are out in nature are right to feel that way. The forest and the sunset and the mountain and the waterfall are so big and wonderful that only something really big and really wonderful could have made them. The forest and the sunset and the waterfall are things only God could have made. They are like God's footprints in the world (even though God really has no feet). Seeing all the wonderful and beautiful parts of nature is one way we know that God is real.

Now, some folks say, "Wait just a minute! The forest is not made by God. It's just made by lots of seeds growing into trees. The sunset is not made by God. It's just made by the setting sun shining through dust in the air. The mountain is not made by God. It's just made by the earth pushing up a lot of dirt. And the waterfall is not made by God. It's just made by water falling off a rock." Now, people who say these things are not looking back far enough. If they asked, "Where did the seeds come from that made the forest, and the dust that made the sunset, and the dirt that made the mountain, and the water that made the waterfall?"

13

they would start going back and back and back into what made what. Of course, trees made the seeds that grew into the forest, and those trees came from seeds of older trees, which came from even older seeds and back and back until you come to the first seed that made the first tree. Now who made that first seed? If it was an older tree, you are still going back and back and you have to stop somewhere with a seed that was put here by God somehow, someway.

God is the one who made the forest, not by making the trees that are in the forest now, but by making the first seed for the first tree that ever was. And then nature took over and made lots of new seeds and new trees by using God's plan for making new stuff out of old stuff. And the same thing happened with the sunset. God made the first dust and the first sun. And the same with the mountain. God made the first dirt. And the same with the waterfall. God made the first water, and then nature took over by using God's plan for making new stuff out of old stuff. God is the only one who is big enough and strong enough and smart enough to make all the first stuff which made everything. This is what we mean when we say that God made the world. God does not plant every forest, but God made the first seeds for the first forest, and God made the plan which makes every forest grow forever and ever.

Some scientists find God when they do their scientific things because they see that only God could have made nature and all the stuff in nature. Albert Einstein, one of the greatest scientists who ever lived, said that his work in science was just "tracing the lines which flow from God."

Scientists know what happens to stuff once it's here. Some scientists think that all the stuff in the world was once squashed into a little package which exploded with a Big Bang! After it exploded, these scientists think that some of the exploded stuff stuck together and made the planets and stars and rocks which we see all around us on earth and in space. The question is, who made the package of stuff that exploded? We believe that God is the only one big enough and smart enough and strong enough to make the stuff which blew up and became everything. God is the stuff maker of the world, because stuff does not make itself. Someone has to make stuff, and that stuff maker has to be very powerful and very smart. Also, the one who made the stuff that started the world cannot be made of stuff. If the stuff maker was made of stuff, then you could ask, "Who made the stuff in the stuff maker?" And if somebody made the stuff in the stuff maker, that somebody would be the real God. Being God means that you make everything and nobody makes you.

Anyway, seeing the stuff in nature and learning that only God could have made nature is one way we learn that God is real even though we can't see or touch or hear or taste or smell God. Nature is something that only God could have made.

2

IS GOD REAL?
PART 2—OUR INSIDE VOICE

Another thing that only God could have made and that shows us that God is real is something inside each one of us. Some people call it our conscience. Some people call it our morals. We call it our inside voice. Our inside voice is the voice that tells us the right thing to do. Our inside voice is what helps us choose between doing the right thing and doing the wrong thing. Our inside voice tells us not to hurt, not to cheat, and not to steal.

Human beings are the only beings with an inside voice, a voice that tells them the right thing to do. Choosing between right and wrong is something that only people can do. Animals just do what they want to do. Animals can't decide between right and wrong. That's the big difference between animals and people (plus the fact that we don't have tails, horns, fins, or fur!).

We have a friend who has a parakeet named Woody who bites people all the time. Woody isn't a bad bird, he just likes to bite. Being a bird, he can't understand that biting people hurts them and is wrong. You have to be a person to know that biting people is wrong. How do we know this? Well, our parents taught us, and their parents taught them, and so forth and so on.

But where did all this teaching from parent to parent begin? It began when people began and when God decided that people would be made special and different from any other animal. At that moment God put an inside voice into us, and from that moment we have been able to know the difference between right and wrong. From that time to this time we have been different from all God's other creatures.

Our inside voice is a very special gift from God. It is something that only God could have given us. No other animal could have taught us about right and wrong because no other animal knows about right and wrong. Once, we looked more like monkeys than like people and monkeys don't know right from wrong. No, the only place where the inside voice could have come from is God. By listening to our inside voice, and by doing the good things it tells us to do, we become more like God than like ani-

17

mals. When we don't listen to our own inside voice, you know what happens. We become more like animals than like God.

Now, because of this special gift from God of an inside voice, we have to make choices. We have to choose every day between doing the right thing and doing the wrong thing. Our inside voice is right there inside of us telling us the right thing to do, but we are the ones who must choose to listen to that voice and do the good thing, or not listen to that voice and do the bad thing.

You know how and when your inside voice speaks to you. Let's say you go into a candy store to buy a chocolate bar and the person who takes your money gives you back too much money. This is his or her mistake, but it isn't your money! As soon as you see that you have been given too much money, if your inside voice is working it will say to you, "What are you waiting for! Give back the extra money! It's not yours!"

Now, we can choose not to listen to that voice and keep the money and buy more candy with it, or we can listen to the voice and return the money. It's our choice. Our inside voice can tell us the right thing to do, but our inside voice cannot make us do the right thing. God wants us to choose to listen to our inside voice. Later in this book we will talk about why God wants us to choose and why God does not *make* us listen to our inside voice. For now, just always try to listen to that voice and remember that it is a very special gift from God. It is in you because of God. It is in you because God loves you and God wants you to do the right thing.

The newspapers sometimes have stories of people who find lots of money and return it to the real owners. Those people are really listening to their inside voices! The more money you find, the harder it is to listen to the voice, but the voice is always there telling you the right thing to do. The only one big enough and good enough and smart enough and strong enough to put inside voices into every single human being is God.

IS GOD REAL?
PART 3—THE BIBLE

Another way we know that God is real is by reading the Bible. The Bible is not one book; it is a bunch of books. And each book of the Bible has stories to tell. The Bible that Jewish people read is called the Hebrew Bible (or the *tanach*). The Bible that Christian people read has books from the Jewish Bible, plus a bunch of other books called the New Testament. What all the stories in all the books in the Bible teach us in one way or another is that God is real. The Bible is another way we know that God is really real.

The stories in the books of the Bible are not like any other stories. By reading these stories, we learn about God. We learn about what God wants us to do. We learn about how God loves us. By reading Bible stories, we learn about the people who lived before us. We learn stories that teach us about what really matters in life. Other books are good but the Bible is more than good, more than great. The Bible is one of the ways God chose to speak to people. The Bible is one of the ways we know that God is real.

Some people say that the Bible was written down by God, and others say that it was written down by people who felt God's presence and listened to God. Whatever way it happened, the Bible is very special to Jews and Christians because it is a way for us to know what God wants us to do and a way for us to learn about God.

Why do you think that people like to read the Bible more than any other book? We don't get sick and tired of hearing Bible stories. We read the Bible when we pray to God, and we study the Bible to learn its lessons. No other book does this for us. The reason is that God's words are in the Bible, and the more we read the Bible, the more we feel close to God.

The Bible teaches us to help people who are poor or sick or hungry or lonely or sad, because every person is made special like God. The Bible teaches us not to steal, because God wants us to work for what we have. The Bible teaches us to keep the earth clean, because God made the earth and put us in charge. These are great things to learn and the Bible teaches us these things.

No other books in the world teach, help, and

direct us like the books of the Bible. This is why we believe that the Bible came to us from God. People who love the Bible have different ideas about how it came to us from God, but many people who love the Bible believe that it came to us somehow, some way, from God. When we read the stories in the Bible, we believe that we are reading something that only God could have written or that only God could have told to people who wrote it down. Whichever way it happened, the Bible is another way we know that God is real.

So let us think back to these first three chapters. Mother Nature, the inside voice, and the Bible are ways we know that God is real. If you are looking for God, there are ways you can know that God is real even though you can't see or hear or touch or smell God.

Now, what you must remember is that some people are not looking for God, and some people don't think that God is real. Even if you tell them that nature, their inside voice, and the Bible are things that only God could have made, these people may still not believe that God is real. What do you do about that?

Well, there is not much you can do. We have found that there is no way to bring people closer to God if they really don't want to be. There is no way to make people believe that God is real if they don't want to. Remember that God is invisible, and God is not like anything else. People who don't believe in what they can't see or touch or taste or smell or hear may never believe that God is real. But there are lots of invisible things that are really real. Feelings are invisible, but feelings are real. When you love somebody, your love for that person is invisible, but it is real. Love is invisible, but real; so are pain and courage, so are patience and goodness. Many things are real but invisible and God is one of them, but God is not like anything else that is invisible and real. God is one of a kind. God is not like anyone or anything else. And nothing is like God.

So you may not be able to teach people about God if they don't want to learn. That's okay. Don't worry. People change, and God is always waiting to love them.

Trying to get some people to believe that God is real is kind of like trying to get somebody to want to play the kazoo. If that person thinks that the kazoo is a dumb thing that makes silly music, then nothing you say is going to make any difference. Wanting to find God and wanting to play the kazoo are a lot alike. You either want to, or you don't.

This book is for people who want to!

4

WHERE DOES GOD LIVE?

God does not live everywhere. God could live everywhere, but for a very good reason God decided to live in only part of everywhere.

Here's how it is. God *is* everywhere in the world, but God *lives* only in people who let God live in them. The world cannot choose to keep God out, but people can choose to keep God out. That is why God is everywhere in the world, but lives only in people who let God live in them.

What do we mean when we say that God is everywhere in the world? If we picked up a handful of dirt and looked really close, would we see God in there between the old leaves and the bubblegum wrappers? No, silly! God lives in the world the way a watchmaker lives in a watch or the way a potter lives in his clay.

When we look at a watch we can sort of see the watchmaker. The watch teaches us things about the watchmaker. If the watch keeps good time, and if the watch is beautiful, then we say that the watchmaker is very good. It's the same with a clay pot. When we see a pot, or hold it in our hands, we learn things about the potter. That is the way that the potter lives, not *in* the pot but *through* the pot—through the design of the pot and through the way it was made. If the pot does not leak, and is beautiful, and is the right shape to hold what it is supposed to hold, then we say that the potter is a good potter.

The way the watchmaker lives in the watch and the way the potter lives in the pot is kind of the way God lives in the world. God made the world, and God made the plan that keeps the world running. By looking at the world and the way it runs, we can learn things about God. God made the world so beautiful and gave it a plan for running right which is such a great plan that we say God is a great world maker, and so God lives in the world.

The world is like God's watch or God's pot. By seeing how the planets spin around and do not go crashing into each other, by seeing how bees find the right flower, by seeing how the stuff on earth is the same as the stuff everywhere else, by seeing how the waves come to the shore, by seeing how plants grow, by seeing how animals are born, by seeing how the sun sets and comes up again, by seeing how the stars come out at night, and by seeing just how things work the way they should, we can see that God is one terrific watchmaker and one great potter. We feel God living in all the living things of the world, and we see God's plan working in every corner of the world. That is what we mean when we say that God is in the world everywhere and all the time.

People are in the world, but we are not like anything else in the world. Everything else works by God's plan all the time. The planets can't decide not to spin around through space. The bees cannot decide not to go searching for flowers. The waves cannot decide not to come into the shore. But people are different. God made us different. We can choose to live by God's plan for our lives, or we can choose not to live by that plan. Later on in this book we will talk about why God made us this way, but for now we just need to remember that people are different from all other things in the world. We can choose to keep God out of our lives.

God wants to live inside all of us, and really God does live inside all of us (remember the inside voice we talked about!). When we follow God's plan for us, which is to be good and kind and clean and help other people and all the other animals, then God lives in us all the way. But when we do bad things and hurt people and mess up the world, we are choosing to push

26

God out of our lives. When we do bad things, we are saying to God, "I don't want you to live in me!" This is very sad. But God waits all the time for us to follow God's plan. Unless we are very, very bad, God always is in us, talking to us through the inside voice and helping us to decide to do the right thing. But all of this is our choice. People are not like watches. If a watch is built right, it runs right. We are built right, but we can choose not to run right. Because people are different from the other things in the world, God cannot live in us unless we let God in. And we let God in when we are good. The better we live, the kinder we are, the more good things we do for other people, the more God lives in us. And that's what we mean when we say that God lives everywhere in nature, but only in those people who let God live in them.

What part of our body does God live in? Well, no one part exactly. God does not live in our noses, or between our toes, or inside our head or under our skin. God lives in a part of us we call our soul. Our soul is the part of us where we let God in, the part of us where we feel God living in us, and the part of us where the inside voice comes from that tells us the right thing to do.

Everybody has a soul, but some people have trouble feeling their soul. Doing bad things makes it hard for you to feel your soul. It's kind of like when you go out into the cold and stay outside for a long time. After a while, the cold makes it hard for you to feel the tips of your toes or the ends of your fingers. You know they are there, but when you get really cold you can't feel them. Well, bad things do to your soul what the cold does to your toes. Doing bad things makes it hard for you to feel your soul. But don't worry! When you do good things you feel your soul right away. Just think back to the way you felt the last time you did something wonderful for somebody else. You felt good inside. Well, that place inside you where you felt good was your soul. You feel it every time you do the right thing.

If you have not felt your soul lately, it might mean that you have not been doing enough good things for other people. When you love people, when you help people, when you work to clean up the world, your soul warms up right away and you can feel God living in you right away. That feeling is so terrific that once you feel it you will want to feel it all the time. And you know what? You can!

The part of us we call the soul does not die when we die. We will talk more about this in the chapter on Elmo the hamster later in this book. Our souls live in our bodies when we are alive. When we die, our souls live with God. That's the deal God makes with us. As long as we are alive, and try to do good things, God lives in us. But when we die, we live in God. It is a very, very good deal.

5

WHAT DOES GOD LOOK LIKE?

Looking *for* God is easy. Looking *at* God is impossible.

We have learned already that God lives everywhere in the world and in people who let God live in them. We can see things everywhere that only God could have made. But we can't see God anywhere for one very big and very simple reason: GOD IS INVISIBLE. We can't see God because God is not a thing, and God has no shape. It's really simple. We can only see things which have edges, and God has no edges.

Everything we can see has edges. People and birds and dogs and boats and trees all have edges, and so we can see just where they start and just where they stop. But God does not stop anywhere. God lives everywhere in nature and everywhere *we* let God in. When you live everywhere, you have no edges because everywhere has no edges. Really, it's very simple. God is everywhere, so God can't have any edges that would divide the place where God is from the place where God isn't. If you could see God, God would probably be so huge that God would block your view of everything else. So when you really think about it, it is pretty good news that God has no edges.

Many people don't like the fact that God is invisible. They want to look *at* God, not just look *for* God. Some folks think that if God is invisible maybe God is not really real. But we know that God is really real. As we said before, we know lots of things (like love) that are invisible but real. God is also invisible but real. We just have to get used to the idea that God is one of those really invisible things that we can't look *at*, we can only look *for*.

Looking for God is different from looking at God. Looking for God is trying to feel close to God. Looking for God is doing things God wants us to do. Looking for God is asking God for help when we need help and feel weak. Looking for God is easy because God is always waiting for us. Looking at God is impossible because God is invisible.

Why do people want to look at God? Well, probably because of love. People want to see what they love, and people love God. You should know that the closest we can come to looking at God is when we look at each other. It says in the Bible that we are all made in the "image of God." Now, since God is not a person, we know that being made in the "image of God" does not mean that if we have a big toe then God has a big toe, too. What being made in the image of God means is that God has made each and every one of us special like God. We are as close to God as any living thing, closer even!

What makes us special is our soul, that part of us where God lives. Our souls make us special like God, and every person no matter what color, no matter what size, no matter what age, has a soul and is made special like God. No person is more special than any other person.

It is just terrific and really amazing how God has made each of us special in the same way, even though each of us looks different. The picture of Abraham Lincoln is on every penny, and every penny looks the same. Well, the picture of God is on every person but every person does not look the same. How terrific is that? This is one of the most wonderful things God ever did. This way nobody can say that anybody is more special than anybody else. Each of us is made special like God in just the same way. Nobody more than anybody else. Even though the colors of our skin are different and the shape of our eyes and the curliness of our hair are all different, we are all special like God in just the same way. Even though some of us can see and some of us can't, even though some of us can hear and others can't, even though some of us can run and others can't, we are all special like God in just the same way.

So whenever you see another person walking along the street, you should think, "There goes somebody special walking down the street." If you think this way, it will be impossible to hurt that person or cheat him or make him feel bad, because he is special like God. All of us are special and that is the main reason we must be kind to each other, and respect each other, and not hurt each other. It is our way of being respectful of God. It is our way of showing God that we know that everybody is loved.

Oh, by the way, God is not a guy. Many kids start out thinking that God is a big, old guy with a long white beard floating on the clouds and watching us. This way of thinking about God is wrong because remember that God is invisible and has no edges. It is also wrong because it makes girls think that God likes guys more than girls, and this is not true. So God is not a guy. Remember that! God is also not a girl. And definitely, God is not a thing!

So what do we call God when we are praying to God, or writing about God, or even thinking about God? We think that calling God *He* or *Him* when we are talking, praying, or thinking about God is wrong, because God is not a guy. Also, calling God *She* or *Her* is wrong because God is not a girl, either. God is not a person of any kind, or color, or shape. And, of course, calling God *It* won't work because God isn't a thing. God isn't like a toaster. If you speak English, you use the words *he/him*, *she/her*, and *it* a lot, and so it is very easy to give people the wrong ideas about God. In this book, whenever we talk about God we just use the name "God." We know that this makes for some funny sentences like, "God said that God wanted God loving people, whom God loves, to do God's works." If you wrote that kind of sentence in English class, your teacher would put a red line through it, but in this book, that is the only choice we have. He/Him and She/Her and It are out. So looking *for* God is easy, but looking *at* God is impossible.

Whenever we replace God with something else in our life, that something else is called an idol. Making idols is a bad idea because idols keep us from finding God. In the old days, people carved idols out of wood or stone and prayed to them instead of to God. Today people still make idols, but they usually don't make them out of wood or stone. For some folks, money is an idol. They "worship" money. They will do anything to get money, and all they care about is money. Money has replaced God in their lives. Money has become their *idol*. So be careful. Idols keep you from finding God. Idols take God's place in your life, and nothing and nobody should take God's place in your life. Not nothing! Not nobody!

=== 6 ===

DOES GOD MAKE MIRACLES?

Miracles are weird, and weird things are always hard to explain. Miracles happen when God changes nature to help people. The Bible is full of stories about miracles. The way the Red Sea split in half and the children of Israel walked right through on dry land is a Bible miracle nearly everybody has heard of, but there are lots more miracles in the Bible. Sticks turn into snakes, water turns into blood, frogs fall from the sky, the sun stops in the sky, blind people see, deaf people hear, crippled people walk, and more. And more.

Miracles confuse a lot of people because they don't understand how these things could have happened. Some people who do not think that God is real (and even some who do) will not feel good about God until they understand about miracles. Scientists tell us that miracles can't happen. So, many people think that if you love God and love the Bible, you have to go against science, or that if you believe in science you have to go against the Bible and God.

We think that with miracles you have two choices: you can believe that miracles are weird, but real; or you can believe that miracles are weird, but not real. Whatever you believe about miracles, you can love God and find God and you can still learn everything that science has to teach you.

The first choice you have with miracles is that they are weird, but real. God is definitely strong enough and smart enough to do them. The plan of the world is a plan God made, so if God wanted to change the plan a few times to help people, God could do it. In fact, God is the only one who could do it for sure. Maybe those miracles we read about happened just the way it says in the Bible. Maybe we are just not smart enough to figure out why or when or how God decides to make a miracle.

Miracles are not the only thing God does that we don't understand. We don't understand the shape of the universe. We don't understand how life started. We don't understand why people fall in love. Lots of things are real that we do not understand. Miracles may be one of those things. Don't forget, we are nowhere near as smart as God. Maybe God makes miracles to teach us that we will never figure out everything about how the world works. Or everything about how God works. It is okay to not understand everything God does. It is amazing we know as much as we do know, but there is a lot about God we don't know and can't know. The main thing is that God is smart enough and strong enough to make miracles if God wants to, and the fact that we don't understand why or how does not matter very much. This is one choice you have in thinking about miracles, that they are weird but real.

The second choice you have in thinking about miracles is that miracles are weird, but not real. Maybe God never really made any miracles, but people invented them to make God seem even more wonderful. Maybe something terrific did happen, and when the storytellers told about it, it got made into a miracle even though nothing against the laws of nature ever happened. Maybe what did really happen was so special and came at such a good time that the people who told the story of what happened made up some weird stuff to make it seem even more special. You know how sometimes we remember things differently from the way they happened? Golfers do that a lot. So do fishermen.

Let's take the big miracle of the splitting of the Red Sea. Maybe the miracle of the splitting of the Red Sea happened this way: The children of Israel ran out of Egypt just as it says in the

Bible, but they got out by running through a mushy swamp. They got through the mush because they were all walking on foot. When Pharaoh tracked them down and chased them through the swamp with his heavy chariots with their heavy horses, the chariots and horses got stuck in the mushy swamp because they were so much heavier than the people who were walking on foot.

Maybe, after many years of telling this story around the campfires, the mushy swamp story turned into a splitting of the Red Sea story, in which God made a big sea divide right down the middle with a wall of high water on one side and a wall of high water on the other side. Maybe God didn't want people to invent a miracle out of a mushy swamp story, but maybe the people did it anyway, to make the story bigger and to make God seem even more powerful. Maybe.

We believe that miracles are real, and we believe that what really matters about miracles is not how they happened but what they mean. Miracles mean that God loves us and will not let us down. The stories of miracles teach us that sometimes, for reasons we cannot know and do not understand, God helps us out of a jam. But miracles also teach us not to sit around like lumps waiting for God to make a miracle for us. We have to do our best to help ourselves and others get out of the mushy swamps we get ourselves into. God wants us to do that, and then, maybe someday, when the Red Sea splits again, we won't be so surprised.

And here's another thing about miracles. Maybe we should be looking for smaller miracles. You know, the miracles that happen when somebody who was not supposed to get better, gets better; the miracles where somebody in a horrible car wreck comes out without a scratch; the miracles where a falling rock just misses your car; the miracles where people live happily ever after; the miracles where you wake up and everything in you is working just fine; the miracles where bees find the right flowers, and birds find the right nests; and the miracles where people who once hated each other find love for each other and the hate disappears.

Maybe miracles are all around us all the time. Now, that would really be weird! Maybe if we just stop looking for the Red Sea to split, or frogs to fall from the sky, we might see all the weird and wonderful miracles God makes all around us every day. Maybe.

7

WHEN MY PET HAMSTER ELMO DIED, DID HE GO TO HEAVEN?

Thinking about heaven is kind of like looking at a puzzle with some of the pieces missing. The puzzle is how God loves us. We know about how God loves us while we are alive; God gives us food to eat and people to love and good things to do. But we don't know and we can't know how God loves us after we die, until we die. And when that happens, we won't be able to phone home. What happens after we die is the part of the puzzle that is missing when we are alive.

You know, when you are putting together a picture puzzle, and you have a bunch of pieces, and some are still in the box, you can still make a good guess about how the puzzle will look when all the pieces are in the right place.

Heaven fits into the puzzle of how God loves us. It fits just right.

We know that God is the most powerful, the most good, the most loving, and the smartest being in the whole universe. We also know that God has made each of us in God's image, which means that God has made each of us special like God. We also know that the part of us where we feel special like God is called our soul.

Now, the part of us where we feel special like God is kind of like a gift from God. It is a gift that helps us to feel special like God. Maybe you could think of it as a pretty balloon that floats along at the end of a string that is tied to our wrist. As long as we are alive, the balloon bounces along with us and tells everybody that the person holding this balloon is special like God. The balloon is tied to our wrist our whole life long. When we are walking down the street and when we are sitting in our house, the balloon is there. When we wake up and when we lie down to sleep the balloon is there. The balloon never loses air, and the string never breaks.

Then one day when God decides it is time for our bodies to die, our bodies die. It is like the string breaking on the balloon. When our bodies die, our souls float back to God to live some more in a new way. It is like the balloon flying up higher and higher into the sky when it is let loose. The balloon is our soul, and the place the balloon goes is called heaven. Well, it is called "heaven" by Christians. Jews call the same place "the world to come." When we die, it is just our bodies that die. Our souls do not die; they just return to God.

God does not die, and our soul is the part of us that is like God, and so our soul does not die. But it must leave the body because the body definitely dies and, in time, it becomes a part of the earth again. So the soul, which does not die, must go somewhere to live, and even though we can't see that somewhere until we die, we have a good reason to believe that it is there with God. Heaven or the world to come is the piece of the puzzle about how God loves us which fits right in to make the picture of our life complete.

You see, a God who loves us as much as God loves us, and who is that smart and that powerful, would not let our souls wander around with nothing to do. After we die, God wants to keep our love alive and bring our souls home. The body is the old home of the soul, and heaven, or the world to come, is the new home. As we said before, when we are alive, God lives in us, and when we die we live in God. It fits the puzzle, even though we won't be able to put the piece into its place until our body dies and our soul goes to heaven. Heaven is the missing piece of the puzzle about how God loves us forever and ever.

Now, even though heaven fits into the puzzle, we don't know and we can't know what the piece of the puzzle called heaven really looks like. Most people think of heaven as God's home address. We know that God lives everywhere in nature and everywhere we let God in, but the idea that heaven is God's home is in a lot of people's minds. They talk about heaven the same way they talk about beautiful places on earth, except that the weather is better up there, and there are no angels down here.

Maybe heaven is like that, but maybe it isn't. We have to be careful not to say things we don't know for sure. We can talk about God for sure because we can see things that only God could have made, so we know that God is really real. But heaven has to be a missing piece of the puzzle because we are alive, and there are things we have to be alive to know, but there are also things we can know only in dying. Heaven is one of those things we know about only when we die.

We also don't know what our soul feels like when it leaves our body when we die. Can it still hear or see or feel or touch or taste things? We don't know for sure, but we think so. Your soul is the part of you that makes you special, and your soul is the part of you that feels what is right to do and tells you what is right to do, so probably the soul still feels those things when it leaves your body. God loves us in such a special and forever way that when our bodies die, God's love for us does not die, and something wonderful and new and amazing happens to our souls.

Also, nobody knows for sure who gets into heaven or the world to come, and who does not. Some people believe that everybody gets in. Some people believe that only good people get in. One thing is for sure. If you do good things just to get into heaven and not just because they are good things, you have missed the whole idea of heaven. Heaven is not a bribe to do good things, the way your parent gives you money to wash the car. Heaven is a place where our souls go home to God after our bodies die.

Also, nobody knows if there are animals in heaven. Nobody knows for sure if animals have souls. An animal definitely doesn't have a soul exactly like our soul because it can't decide between good and bad. But animals are made by God and loved by God in a special kind of way, too. Is God's love for animals big enough to bring them to heaven? We believe that God also loves animals enough to do this wonderful thing for them, too. And if we are right, you may see the soul of your pet hamster Elmo again when your soul gets to heaven or the world to come. You may also see the souls of the goldfish that you flushed down the toilet, so be prepared! If hamsters have souls and if souls need exercise, then Elmo might just turn up again running on his little hamster wheel in heaven. And if Elmo is there, one thing is for sure. Elmo will not need a cage, because when Elmo gets to heaven, he won't want to run away.

8

DOES GOD KNOW WHAT I'M THINKING OR WHAT I'LL DO?

Let's say you have a crush on somebody who doesn't even know you're alive. You really want that person to love you, but no matter what you do or what you say, nothing happens. Now, let's say a fairy godmother flies into your room one night, and offers you a magic love potion in a bottle. All you have to do is get the person you love to drink the potion, and he or she will love you forever. That day, at lunch, you see the person you love, and you have a chance to pour the love potion into that person's orange juice. You reach into your pocket, you take out the bottle. You remove the cork, and then all of a sudden you ask yourself, "Do I really want this person to love me because of a love potion?" You know that he or she will

44

not really be loving you because he or she decided to love you. Knowing that makes all the difference. If you have any sense, you will try to return the potion to the fairy godmother on her next visit to your room.

If God wanted to, God is smart enough and strong enough to give a magic potion to every person so that each of us would do exactly what God wanted us to do every day and in every way. BUT, if God did that, then what we did would not be our own free choice. And although God wants us to love God, God wants us to choose to do it just the way we choose to love anyone else—by our own free choice. God could have made us like robots, doing whatever God wants whenever God wants it, but then we would not be the kinds of people we are, and what we did would not count, because the only things that count are the things you decide to do with your own free choice.

What makes our love for God so wonderful is what makes all love so wonderful. We decide to love God; nobody decides for us, and that's the kind of love God wants from us. When you think about it, that's the kind of love we want from each other. We can decide to love each other or not to love each other. When we decide not to love each other, all sorts of bad things happen. Wars happen. But even wars and the other bad things are worth something. They teach us to learn from our bad choices. God

45

wants our love to count, and love does not count unless it is a free choice.

People want to count. People want to be free. That is what God wants for us, too. And that is why it is so terrible when some dictator or bad leader takes away people's freedom. Learn about the world and you will see that people try and run away from places where they are not free. They run as fast as they can to places where they can choose what they want to do. God made each and every one of us free, so don't let anybody take your freedom away. And if you ever have a chance to help people run away from a place where they are not free, you should definitely help them run away. God wants all of us to be free!

Being free means that we make our own choices and our choices count. God does not make our choices for us. Through our inside voice, God tells us the right thing to do. God tells us to love each other. God put an inside voice into each of us which tells us the right thing to do, but God can't make us do the right thing. God might even know what we are thinking and God might even know what we will choose to do, but God does not choose for us. Only we choose what we will do. That is what it means to be free. If God made us do the right thing, then what we did would not really count. It would be like drinking the love potion. No, God wants us to really choose because that is the only way that what we do will really count.

Being free is a terrific gift from God but it does not always make us happy. Sometimes we really don't want to be free. Sometimes we want people to make our choices for us, because some choices are so hard. Not cheating on a test when cheating will get you a better grade is a hard choice. Telling on a friend when he or she does a bad thing is a hard choice. Being friends with somebody whom nobody likes is a hard choice. Knowing which charity to give your money to when you don't have a lot of money to give away is a hard choice. You know that choices are sometimes hard. But making choices is what makes us grow up.

Sometimes we will make the wrong choice. That's for sure! We are only human beings. We are not as smart as God, but we are free like God. Don't worry about making bad choices. It is going to happen to you sooner or later.

Now, when it happens and you make a bad choice, you must first learn how to say, "I'm sorry!" to any people you have hurt by your bad choices. If they are good people, they will understand that they have made bad choices, too, and that they should forgive you. If they don't forgive you, that's their bad choice and not yours.

The next thing you need to learn is that saying you are sorry is not enough. You must try to fix up the bad things you did. This is sometimes very hard to do. It can be like trying to put spilled milk back into a bottle, but you

47

must try. Saying you are sorry is just not enough. When you do something bad, you must try to do something good to fix it.

The main thing is that when you choose the wrong thing, you must be brave enough and honest enough to say what you did. You chose it. You did it, and only you can fix it up if it was wrong. Choosing to do the wrong thing is bad enough. Don't make it worse by saying that it was not your fault.

Learning how to say, "I am sorry for that bad choice I made!" is one of the ways we grow up. Learning how to ask people to forgive us is one of the ways we keep love alive. If you can't say "I'm sorry," and if you can't say "Please forgive me," then you can't grow up. If you can't say those things, you can't keep love alive between you and your family, or between you and your friends. But you should know this: Once you say you are sorry and once you really try to fix up the bad things you have done, God will forgive you even if people don't. God will make you feel better even if people don't, and God will give you the strength to say you are sorry again, even if people don't.

Don't worry if you find that choosing the right thing and doing the right thing is hard. What you must always remember is that there are always people around who are very good at choosing and who are very good at teaching you how to choose. These people are priests and rabbis and ministers and parents and teachers and friends and sometimes even strangers. The world is filled with people who will teach you how to choose the right thing, but you must look for them and you must let them help you. God would never ask us to choose so many things without giving us so many teachers.

Choosing and being free is a wonderful gift from God, and using the gift makes us all grow up. That's how God made us, and aren't we glad that God made us just that way!

═══ 9 ═══

IF GOD IS SO GOOD, WHY IS THERE SO MUCH BAD?

Bad choices! That's the main thing. People make bad choices, and it makes the world terrible. But don't blame it on God. Most bad things in the world happen because people are making bad choices.

Let's start with pollution. Pollution is a bad thing because it spills poisons into our air and water and food, and the poisons hurt us. But is pollution God's fault? No! Pollution is a bad choice people have made not to care about the dirty air and dirty water. Pollution is our bad choice to be selfish, and greedy, and dirty. It is our bad choice not to care about the earth, or the people who are born after us and who will have to clean it all up.

Or take murder. Murder is another bad thing

that is not God's fault. Murder happens when people kill each other because they are angry and forget that other people are special the way God is special. Murder is a choice to settle arguments by killing and not by talking. Murder is a terrible choice, but it is not God's choice.

Some diseases are even caused by bad choices. Nobody makes you smoke cigarettes, but if you do, you have made a bad choice that could make you very sick. Nobody makes you eat food with lots of fat and sugar in it, but if you do, you have made a bad choice, and your heart may get sick. Nobody makes you take drugs, but if you do, you have made a bad choice, and you could get sick, or even die, from a whole bunch of terrible diseases that come from using drugs.

So, a whole lot of the bad stuff in the world comes from people making bad choices. We already know that God can't stop us from making bad choices without taking away our special gift—the gift of the freedom to choose between good and evil. Is it God's fault that so many people make so many bad choices?

There is one problem. Some bad stuff does not seem to come from bad choices. Take hurricanes. What bad choice did people make that caused a hurricane? But hurricanes kill people and flood their homes, and blow their stuff around. Hurricanes are bad, but they don't seem to come from a bad choice. Or what about babies who die of strange diseases? The babies

51

who die are too young to make any choices. Are hurricanes and babies who die God's fault?

Maybe. But first, let's think about hurricanes. What makes hurricanes bad is not the wind or the rain, but the fact that people live right where hurricanes come ashore. If they had chosen to live in Colorado, they would never be hit by a hurricane. Hurricanes are just big winds and are not really bad themselves. They are just bad if you get in their way, and some people live where hurricanes are. Now, we know that sometimes people don't have much of a choice about where they live. If you are a fisherman, you can't really decide to live in Colorado, because it would take you too long to get to work in the morning. The point is that hurricanes are not really bad. Just getting in their way is bad.

The death of babies is the saddest thing. We don't know why many babies die. We know that sometimes babies die for the same reasons adults die. Maybe some of the pollution in our air and water that gives cancer to some of us, also gives it to some babies through their mother while they are inside their mother waiting to be born. We know that if a woman who has a baby growing inside her does not take care of herself, and eat right, and get enough sleep, and not smoke or take drugs or drink alcohol, then the baby may become sick or even die. Some babies die because of bad choices made by their mothers or by the nation

52

where the mothers live which does not help them take care of the babies growing inside of them.

But not every baby dies because of a bad choice, even though some of them die that way. Sometimes babies die for no reason we know. They just die. We know that some baby animals die because they are too sick, and we know that the same thing happens to baby people, but we don't know why. God seems very mean to take a baby who has made no bad choices and whose mother has done all the right things.

Sometimes millions of people are killed in a war. They are killed because other people don't like their religion or their skin color or the country they came from or how they think a country should be ruled. God seems very mean to allow millions of people to die who have not made any bad choices.

What can we say about the bad stuff that seems to come from God? The first thing we can say is that it is all right not to know why God allows things to happen which seem mean. We are not God, and we don't always know why God lets bad things happen to good people, but it's okay not to know. We know that God loves us, and we know that if we do what God has told us to do, the world will be a better place with much less bad stuff in it. But we don't know, and it's okay not to know, why God lets bad stuff happen which is not the result of bad choices.

What we think is that maybe God made the world with holes in it. Not the kinds of holes you fall in and have to climb out of, but the kinds of holes that are like the unfinished parts of a puzzle. The holes are the bad things that God left in the world for us to work on and make better. The holes are the diseases we don't know how to cure yet. The holes are the way we let some people get so poor that they starve and other people get so rich that they don't care about anybody else. The holes are like our homework from God, and if we do our homework we will make the world better.

We know a doctor who decided to become a doctor when she saw a baby die needlessly. She is spending her life trying to fill in a hole God left in the world. We also know a man who is trying to figure out hurricanes, so that he can tell people, long before a hurricane hits the land and blows stuff around, to tie their stuff down and get out of there. Holes in the world are the stuff God gave us to work on. Maybe when we fill in all the holes the only bad stuff will come from bad choices, and maybe we will learn how to make fewer bad choices, too.

One thing is for sure. Nothing bad comes from God. God is too good, too loving, and too wise to make bad stuff just for the heck of it. The bad stuff comes from our bad choices, or from holes in the world which God left for us to fill in. Nothing bad comes from God. But there is a lot of bad around. We know that. You know that. We all know that. So we better get to work before it gets worse. Let's start by making fewer bad choices. That's the main thing.

══ 10 ══

WHY COULDN'T GOD LET GRANDPA DIE FAST WITHOUT PAIN?

Pain is one of the hardest questions. It's not so hard to understand why God lets people die. After all, the world needs room for babies. But what is really hard to understand is why God lets people die with pain. Pain makes dying even harder, and it seems mean of God to make dying harder than it is anyway.

We could all understand why Grandpa was dying. Grandpa was an old man. He had lived a long life, and he had lived long enough to see the children of his children. But why did God let Grandpa suffer so much pain at the end of his life? Why couldn't God just let him die fast and take the pain away from him?

Pain is one of the hardest questions. The first thing to know about pain is that God made pain a kind of warning bell that something is wrong in our bodies. When we feel a pain, it is God's way of telling us, "Check it out!" The tummy pain we feel may be just too much ice cream, or it may be our appendix. The pain in our ear may be just too much rock music, or it may be an infection. So pain is good when it acts as a warning bell for our bodies. Without pain we would not know we had burned our finger on the stove or broken our leg sliding into second base.

But the kind of pain that is hard to understand is the pain that sometimes comes at the end of life. That's when we can't fix what the warning bell tells us is wrong. Some people suffer pain for years before they die. That pain can make their lives, and the lives of those people who love them, terrible. Allowing that kind of pain can make God seem cruel.

Let's think about pain. You remember how some kids really freaked out when they got a shot from the doctor, while other kids didn't. It's the same with adults. Some adults can't stand pain, and others can. We don't know why some kids and adults freak out about pain, and others don't. We can't decide to have pain, or not to have pain, but we can sometimes decide how pain gets to us. If you drop a rock on your toe, you are going to have pain! But you can decide not to freak out. You can decide to accept the pain and try not to let it make you crazy. What we do with pain is a choice God gives us to help us learn how to not get crazy when bad things happen.

The pain that comes from dropping a rock on your foot is outside pain, but there is also inside pain which comes in other ways. When a friend moves away, you feel inside pain. When a grandpa or grandma you loved so much dies, you feel inside pain. When your dog or cat runs away or gets run over, you feel inside pain. Sometimes inside pain is worse than outside pain because it takes longer for it to go away. But even with inside pain, you have a choice. You can think about how sad you are that your friend moved away or your grandpa died or your dog ran away, and you can make yourself feel worse and worse. Or you can think of all the good times you had with that person or with that pet when they were with you. You can try to think happy thoughts about them, and those happy thoughts make the inside pain hurt a little less. The reason we have inside pain is because of the love we felt for that person or that pet. Love hurts when those we love go away. But love is still good, and even though we know that we will have pain whenever we can no longer be with those we love, we still are lucky to be able to love. Love is worth the inside pain, because love's the finest thing around.

So you see that whether pain is inside or outside, you have a choice. You can let pain make you so miserable that you can't think of anything else. Or, you can learn that the pain is a feeling that will not go away, but that you can choose to control more than you first thought. That is a lesson God wants us to learn. That may be one of the reasons God lets us feel inside and outside pain.

And another thing about pain. Pain reminds us to be thankful when we don't have it. Sometimes we get selfish without knowing that we are getting selfish. We think that all the good things that happen to us are supposed to happen, and we sometimes think that all the bad things are just a mistake. Pain reminds us just how lucky we are when we don't have pain. Pain can help us not to be selfish about our blessings. Pain can help us to be thankful to God for all the good times we have when we have them.

Pain can also help us to understand people who have to live with pain all the time. Even though nobody wants to have pain, pain can teach us lessons about life which make us more grateful and more wise about things.

We knew somebody who broke her leg and had to use a wheelchair for a while. She learned how hard it was for people in wheelchairs to get into buildings and buses and trains. When she got better she decided to help people who have to use wheelchairs all the time. She helped to get people who don't have to use wheelchairs to listen to those people who do. She convinced them to make it easier for people in wheelchairs to get into and out of places. So next time you are really happy and feeling great and everything is just fine, don't forget to thank God right then, right there. You never know when things are going to change.

Pain can also teach us to look at our life in a new way. Pain can be God's way of reminding us about what really matters, not just all the silly things we think matter but which really don't. Having pain can be like pushing a button to start our lives again. Pain can bring us to God for help in trying to understand things. Pain can bring us to God for help in learning to live with pain. Pain can bring us to God for comfort and for healing. Nobody wants to have pain, but what pain does to us is not always bad.

Pain also gives us the chance to help other people who are in pain. The whole family had to help Grandma take care of Grandpa. We all took time to be together with Grandpa, and we all tried to cheer him up and make him feel as good as he could feel. In that time we all learned what it meant to be a part of a family. In that time we sort of repaid Grandpa for all the love he had given us over the years. Of course, Grandpa didn't want to be repaid, but that is kind of what happened. He gave us love when we were in pain, and now we were giving him love. Pain is not good, but the way pain can help us to learn to help others is good.

Grandpa never seemed to think about himself when he was dying. He always asked about us. "How is school?" "Are you helping Grandma?" Grandpa wanted to know about our little problems when he was facing a great big problem. He wanted to know if Grandma was all right. He loved her so much that his pain got less because of that love. That was a real lesson for all of us. It taught us about love and pain, but mostly it taught us about love. What Grandpa did for Grandma when he was well was what we had to try and do when Grandpa was sick. It seems hard to believe, but out of Grandpa's pain came love. That made the pain easier to get through.

Grandpa told us on the day before he died, "I was never counting on living forever. I was never counting on being rich. I was never even counting on having a lot of friends, but what I always counted on was that my family would love me. God has answered my prayer."

When we saw that Grandpa was thankful to God even though he was in pain and was about to die, it made all of us thankful to God. Grandpa taught us about God, and God helped Grandpa live in love through his last days.

Then we told Grandpa what all people should be able to hear before they die, "We love you, and you will never be alone." Those words helped Grandpa live with the pain, and they helped us live with the pain. That's all that words and love can do, but it's a lot.

Sometimes we learn more from bad things

than from good things, and pain is a bad thing which teaches us a lot. It teaches us not to get crazy when bad things happen. It teaches us to be thankful for all the times when we have no pain, and it teaches us to help other people who must live with pain all the time. God has many, many ways to teach us, and pain is one of the ways.

We need to remember just why we do good deeds. We do good things because they make us feel good. We do good things because we love the person or the animal we are doing them for. We do good things because we believe that God wants us to do good things. All these reasons come from us being the way we are. We are special like God. Good things are the right things to do.

Now, some people do good things for another reason. They think that good things are like coins that they can drop into a piggy bank. They think that they need to store up a certain number of coins in their bank to pay for a ticket to heaven.

Maybe we do need a certain number of good-deed coins to get into heaven or the world to come and maybe we don't. What we know for sure is that if we do good things just to get to heaven, we don't understand what a good thing really is.

A good thing is something we do just because it is good and not because it will get us something else we want. When you really think about it, isn't it kind of selfish to do a good thing just so that you will get a reward for doing it? When you help an old lady across the street, you aren't doing it because you think she will give you a dollar. You are doing it (we hope!) because it is the right thing to do, or because it makes you feel good, or because you think God wants you to help old people when you can. Those are good reasons for doing a good thing. Doing a good thing so that you can get a reward is not bad. It's just not the best reason.

Now, if you learn to do good things just because they are good, and not because you think you will get some terrific reward, then you can also learn *not to do* bad things just because they are bad, and not because you are afraid of getting caught. Being afraid of getting caught is one of the main reasons why some people don't do bad things. They don't want to get caught by their parents, by their teachers, by the cops or by God (who they think of as partly a teacher, partly a parent, and partly a cop). They think that even if a teacher or a parent does not see the bad thing they did, God will see it and God will punish them.

We think that God does see every bad thing

we do. God will do something about these things somehow, someway, after we die. That is another thing we will have to be dead to know, and we can't know much about it while we are alive. Don't be afraid, but don't think that no one sees the bad things you do. God sees them even when nobody else is looking.

What we should all remember when we are alive is that we should have a better reason for not doing bad things than just being afraid of getting caught. If we can do good things just because they are good, then we surely can avoid doing bad things just because they are bad. Doing bad things should give us a bad feeling inside, just like doing good things gives us a good feeling inside.

Also, if we think that good deeds get a reward and bad deeds get punished, then we are going to be very confused, because here on earth many people who do bad things don't get caught and many good people have bad things happen to them. We don't know why this happens. Nobody knows why this happens. But what we do know is that we cannot spend our time counting up who gets rewarded and who gets punished. We need to remember why we do good things and why we don't do bad things, and the reasons for both should have nothing to do with getting rewarded or getting punished.

God is not a cop or scorekeeper. God is more like a teacher or a parent who loves us and wants us to do the right thing for the right reason. We believe that God does see everything, and we believe that God does take care of good people somehow, someway, sometime. But what we believe most of all is that God wants us to learn to do good, just because it is good, and to learn not to do bad, just because it is bad.

Thinking about God as a big cop in the sky who will pull you over and give you a ticket every time you do a bad deed is also a very scary way to think about God. It is hard to love somebody you think is about to arrest you. God wants us to love God. When you love somebody, you want to do what he or she wants you to do. When you fear somebody, you just want to get away! Loving God is the best and only lasting reason to do all the good things God has told us to do.

Look at the world the way it really is. And the way the world really is, is that sometimes we get away with doing a bad thing. But that does not mean that God does not see it, and that does not mean that it is not a bad thing. It just means that for a lot of reasons that don't really matter we got away with a bad thing. We shouldn't have done it, and we shouldn't do it again.

Remember, God really loves us and wants us to do good, just because it is good, and not to do bad, just because it is bad. Not everybody can live with that, but it's the truth. It makes us grow up. No doing the right thing just to get a reward! No not doing bad things just to avoid getting caught! Just do the right thing!

12

IS IT OKAY TO GET ANGRY
AT GOD?

Someday when you feel God has let you down,
you might get angry with God. Don't worry.
It's okay. God can take it, and there is no sense
saying you are not angry when you are angry.
Getting angry with God happens for the same
reason we get angry at people we love. When
you love somebody so much, and you trust them
so much, and you depend upon them so much,
and then they let you down, you get really angry. Getting angry with people you love happens all the time.

Getting angry with people you love is one
sign that you really care about them. It's really
hard to get angry at somebody you don't care
about. It's the same with God. The more we
love God, the more we may have times when

we get angry at God. But getting angry at God is different from getting angry at your little brother for breaking your radio. When you get angry at your little brother, you yell, and scream, and throw things, and run around the house, and then it's all over. Getting angry with God is weird because God doesn't say anything and you don't know where to run or where to throw things or what to do.

Mostly people get angry at God because somebody they love a lot just died. This anger is okay. You loved the person, and he or she died. You know that God is very powerful, and very smart, and you know that God could have let him or her live a little longer. God could have, and nobody knows why God didn't. Why people die when they do is something only God knows. If we were God we would know, but we aren't so we don't.

All we do know (and it's good to remember this when you get angry at God) is that the God who let that person you loved die is the very same God who let that person you loved live. The God who allowed that person to go out of your life is the very same God who put that person into your life. So even when we are angry at God, which is okay, we still have something to thank God for. When you are angry, it is good to remember that. If we blame God for what goes wrong, at least we should thank God for what goes right.

So, it's all right to get angry at God when someone or something you love dies, because it hurts, and because you don't understand why. We should just try to be thankful for every good thing we have and for every good person who is near us for as long as all that goodness lasts.

If the person who died did a lot of good things, we may feel that God is being really unfair, but remember what we said in the last chapter. The good things we do are not like coins in a piggy bank. We don't get more life by doing good things; we just get a better life, a fuller life, a more loving life. God always plays fair, even though we might not see it that way. God is all-knowing, remember, and we are not, because we are not God.

But still and all, it hurts when somebody we love dies. It's okay to feel that hurt. You may feel lousy and you may feel hurt. The hurt happens because the love happened. The bigger the love you had for the person who died, the bigger the hurt.

Some days when the hurt is bad and you really miss somebody whom you loved and who died, and you want the hurt to go away, think of this:

If somebody came to you and told you that he or she could take the hurt away from you but only by wiping out any memory you had of loving that person, would you want that? Would you agree to have all the wonderful, loving memories of that person erased from your brain just so that you would not feel the hurt of their dying? We think you probably would not want

69

to give up love just to get rid of the hurt. We think that most likely you would still want to be loved by that person even though you knew that you would feel a big hurt when that person died. We think that most all of you would take the love *and* take the hurt. Hurt is the price we pay for love when it goes away. The bigger the love the bigger the hurt. Love is so great that it is worth the hurt.

When you take the love and take the hurt that happens when somebody we love a lot dies, you can learn a great lesson. After the biggest part of the hurt passes, you will see that the love never really dies. The person you loved dies but not the love you had for him or for her. You remember the love every day and it still warms you inside the way it always did, and makes you feel special the way it always did. Yes, you feel sad too, when you remember the love of somebody who died, but the love lasts! That is a terrific thing to learn.

So after your anger at God has passed a little, remember what you always knew. Love lasts beyond death, and we don't know, and we can't know, when the people we love will die. So we can wait for it to happen, and then blame God. Or we can wake up every day and thank God for all the people and living things around us we love, and which God has given to us to love for some time ... even though we don't know how long. Remember that death does not end love. Only hate ends love.

13

WHEN I TALK TO GOD, DOES GOD LISTEN?

The important thing about talking to God is not only to listen carefully to what God says to us, but to listen carefully to what we say to God.

Talking to God is praying. The things we say to God are our prayers. Think about your prayers. Some prayers are prayers that ask God for stuff. You may want a new bike, so you ask for the bike in your prayers. You may think, "It can't hurt to ask God to give me this bike. Maybe God will come through." Well, God does hear you, but if you get a bike it will not be from God. You have to buy a bike, and God is not like a checkout clerk in some toy store in the sky. God gives us lots of stuff. God has given us beautiful bodies and a wonderful

world, and all of that is a free gift from God.
When you think about how wonderful the free
stuff is that God has given us, isn't it kind of
greedy and selfish to ask God for more stuff in
our prayers?

Asking God for stuff also makes us forget that
we have to work hard for what we want. Let's
say God did give you the bike. POOF! Well,
later on when you want a car, you might just
think all you have to do is sit back, put your
feet up, and order the model and color you want
from God's big catalog book and POOF! You
would get a car. If God did this for us, God
would be delivering stuff all the time, and
we would become lazy and selfish. We would
not want to work, because we could just be or-
dering up stuff from God the way we call to
order a pizza.

Talking to God about anything that is on
your mind is good, but if the only thing that is
on your mind is getting more and more stuff,
then maybe you ought to change your mind.
Instead of praying to God for a bike, you might
want to work hard, save your money, and buy
one. That's probably what God would tell you,
anyway.

Sometimes people we love get sick, and so we
pray to God to make them well again. This is
a better thing to ask for than a bike, because
at least we are asking God to help somebody
else. We can buy a bicycle, but sometimes we
can't make people well who are sick. We really

do need God's help at those times. And there is nothing wrong with praying to God to ask for that help. But remember, God does not make everybody well who is sick. Maybe the person you love who is sick will get well, and maybe not. God does not tell us who will get well and who won't. But one thing you must always know. God hears every prayer, and God does hear our prayers for someone we love to get better.

We believe that God answers every prayer, but not always in a way we can understand. It's okay not to understand all the ways God answers prayers. We are not God; we just love God and pray to God to tell God about that love, and, sometimes, to ask God's help for those people we love here on earth.

Some prayers do not ask God for anything at all. These prayers are the ones where you thank God for good stuff you already have, or where you remind God how much you love God.

When you thank God for all the good things you already have, you keep yourself from becoming selfish. When you remind God how much you love God you are also reminding yourself. These prayers are great prayers. They are not begging, they are happy, loving talks with God. Such prayers remind us that when we are healthy and when we have a home and food and people to love us, we have been blessed by God. We should thank God every day for all the good things we have been given. And when we pray that way, and when we really think about how many great things we already have, then the fact that we are still waiting for a bike won't seem so bad.

Now, we can understand why God doesn't give us a bike the minute we want one, but why doesn't God give some people a place to sleep, or food to eat, or somebody to love them? There are so many people who are so sick and so sad in the world; it is a big question why God does not help them out. But when you think about it for a minute, it is really a big question for us, and not a big question for God. If God could answer us, this is probably what God would say:

"WHAT!! You want me to help these poor people! Why don't you help them? You have enough money! You have enough food! You have enough people who could hug them and love them. Now get off your rear ends right now and start doing one small thing to feed one hungry person, or clothe one cold person, or shelter one homeless person. They are all your brothers and sisters! I made each of them special! They are all loved by me! How dare you get angry at me for not doing enough when you are not doing enough?

"Your prayers are just fine. Keep on praying, but make sure that when you are finished with your prayers, you go out and do the work in the world which will help make your prayers come true.

"I have given you more than enough blessings to go around! When you share these blessings, you will become better people, and the world will become a better place. You are like my hands, and I want you to spread my blessings everywhere."

And that is probably just about exactly what God would say to us.

=== 14 ===

DOES GOD ALWAYS
LOVE ME?

Yes.

Always.

But it is hard to know this sometimes.

There are many people who get very sad for a long time. All because they think that nobody loves them. They think that there is something wrong with them, or something about them that they should be ashamed of. So they don't feel loved. People who do not feel loved are like plants without water. They shrink up.

Most folks who get sad like that really are loved, but for some reason they just can't feel the love. That is why it is very, very important that we remember always that God loves us just the way we are. God made us special like

God. God made us wonderful and alive. God made us terrific!

Sometimes it is easier to believe that God loves us than it is to believe that people love us. God is never too busy to listen, because God is perfect. But people can be too busy for each other. Sometimes we just get so busy doing what we are doing that we forget the feelings of the human beings around us. Sometimes we forget just how much we all need to feel wanted. We are made special like God, but we are not perfect like God is perfect so we have to try extra hard to remind the people we love that we do really love them all the time, even though we don't say it all the time. So when you think that only God loves you, don't forget that lots of people love you even though they don't say it enough.

Sometimes it is easier to believe that people love us than to believe that God loves us. When somebody we love dies, we sometimes get angry at God. When we see bad things in the world, we sometimes get angry at God. We have already talked about how it is all right to get angry at God during those times, but what God wants us to remember is that the reason we love other people is that they are special to us, and God is the one who brought all that specialness to us, and God is the one who makes love real between each of us. So whether we begin by loving God or begin by loving each other, we must remember that God loves us always, just the way we are.

Now, when we are loved by each other we feel it by a hug or a kiss. God has no lips and God has no arms, so how do we feel God's love? God "hugs" us, too, and God "kisses" us, but they are different hugs and different kisses from the ones we get from each other.

Have you ever walked in the snow and felt a snowflake land on your lips and melt there? That melting snowflake is like a kiss from God. Have you ever felt the wind blow in off the water ahead of the waves and push against you? That wind is like a hug from God. All the wonderful things in the world are like hugs and kisses from God.

God hugs and kisses us through the world, and we should try to keep that world clean, so that when God hugs and kisses our children and their children, the snowflake that melts on their lips will also be pure and clean.

God also hugs and kisses us when we hug and kiss each other. Every time we are good to each other, every time we help each other, every time we are not mean to each other, God is right there making love bigger in the world.

So, God loves us always. We must always remember, even in the times when we are very sad and feel like going out and eating worms (don't forget God made the worms too!), that God's love is right there with us. Anyway, a hug is still a hug and a kiss is still a kiss, whether it comes to us from God or from each other.

God loves you.

Always.

Just the way you are.

=== 15 ===

IF THERE'S ONE GOD,
WHY ARE THERE SO
MANY RELIGIONS?

The reason there are different religions is the same reason there are many paths up a mountain. If the mountain is big enough, there are going to be many paths to the top, because some of the climbers go up one way, and some go up another way. After many years, certain paths up the mountain are used more than others, because the climbers have found that these paths are good paths that take them to the top without getting them lost. But there are always new climbers coming to the mountain, and some of them don't want to climb up using the old paths. So they try new ways. Sometimes they start a good new path to the top, and sometimes they get lost. Starting a new path is hard because you don't know if you will find your way.

Well, you see, the mountain is the place where all people climb who want to find God. The different paths up the mountain are like our different religions. We are the climbers. The top of the mountain is where we meet God. God is happy that there are many paths, because that means everybody gets a chance to see a different part of the mountain. It also means that more people can climb because there are more paths to the top. God is happy that there are many paths to the top of the mountain. God loves all of the climbers, and God helps each one of them in their climbing.

Once, a long time ago, there were no paths up the mountain. Then a bunch of real good climbers came to the mountain. These first climbers were Jews. Sarah, Abraham, Rachel, Moses, Isaiah, and many others. Abraham was the first climber, and Moses was the best climber the Jews ever put on the mountain. The oldest path up the mountain is the path these Jewish climbers made. Jews are still climbing up the mountain on that same path.

After some time, some of the Jewish climbers started a new path up the mountain. These climbers were named Matthew, Mark, Luke, John, Mary, Peter, Paul, James, and many others. They followed a new path that was shown to them by Jesus, whom they believed to be the Son of God. The new path was good. It got to the top of the mountain just like the Jewish path. Time went by, and the new climbers who decided to follow Jesus' path up the mountain called themselves Christians, and their path was used by many people who got to the top of the mountain that way, and who still get to the top of the mountain that way.

Then a climber named Mohammed started up the mountain in his own way. Many people followed him to the top of the mountain on the path he showed them, and these climbers called themselves Muslims.

After many years and many climbers, the old Christian path split up with some Christians climbing one way and other Christians climbing another way, but close by. Some of these new Christian climbers called themselves Protestants, and some called themselves Catholics, and some called themselves Orthodox Christians.

Anyway, all these paths got to the top of the mountain. Now, when the climbers got to the top a wonderful thing happened. They saw that the top of the mountain was heaven and they met God there. As they looked around they saw light, and colors, and lots of families all together. Some of the people on the top of the mountain were old, and some were young. They saw animals on the top of the mountain, and they felt so good inside that they all just started to sing and dance.

The Jewish and Christian and Muslim climbers were surprised and very happy to learn that the mountain was so big that there were climbers coming to the top from all over the mountain. The paths these other climbers followed were different from the Jewish or Christian or Muslim paths but they still got to the top. These other climbers were called Hindus. Then some other climbers who started up the Hindu path and then found their own new path up the mountain were called Buddhists. And there was room for all of them!

On the way up the mountain you may meet climbers who will tell you, "Our path is the only path up the mountain! None of the other paths get to the top. If you want to get to the top of this mountain, you better leave the path you are on and follow our path. If you don't, we know that you will never get to the top."

It is good that these climbers are so happy about their path, but it is not good that they do not want to give other climbers a chance to get to the top of the mountain by their own way. These climbers have forgotten the very most important thing about the mountain: *Many paths lead to the top!* These climbers don't know enough about mountain climbing or enough about the mountain. So if you meet climbers like this on your way up the mountain, try to be patient with them and teach them that many paths lead to the top.

Now, you must remember that not every climber will make it to the top of the mountain.

Some climbers may think that it will take too long to get to the top, and they will give up. Some climbers may think that there is nothing special to see at the top of the mountain, and so they will give up. Some climbers may think that they do not have enough strength to climb, and they will give up. And some will follow wrong paths. But don't you give up! God wants you to get to the top of the mountain. God has put markers all along the paths that lead to the top. Climbing the mountain takes time, but it is fun and you will meet great people on the way up and God will give strength to every climber who really wants to get to the top.

Remember that we are all climbing this mountain together. So when you meet other climbers on a different path, do this: Stop, and then talk to them. Tell them what you have learned on your path. Ask them what they have learned climbing on their path. Don't forget to offer to share some of your food, and teach them some of your climbing songs.

When you must leave them, tell them this: "I am going now to continue my climb up the mountain on the path my fathers and mothers marked out for me. I wish you a good climb on your path. I will pray for you. Thank you for sharing with me the things you have seen. I know we will see more things on the way up. I know the way is steep, but I also know that we will meet someday at the top of this mountain. There we will not be tired. There we will see as far as any person can see. There we will learn as much as any person can learn about God. We will be there together, all of us, climbers, the ones who made it long ago, and the ones who are just making the climb now. God bless you, and good luck in your climb to the top."

16

DOES GOD TALK TO PEOPLE?

God talks to us through tellers. You know, the ones who tell what God wants us to know. They are called prophets, but they are the tellers. Now, over all the time that people have been on planet earth (which, when you study it, is really not that long a time), there have been many tellers who have lived and who have told what God wants us to know.

Tellers come in all shapes and sizes and colors. They can be men, or women, or children, or old people. They can come from any nation and from any religion. Some tellers tell what God wants us to know by speaking words. Some do it by singing. Some do it by painting. Some do it by making music. Because God wants us to know so much, and because God wants us to know it in so many ways, there is always room for new tellers to come along and find a new way to tell us what God wants us to know.

After many years, people have their favorite tellers, and there are teller fan clubs, which are called religions. There are old tellers and there are new tellers, but the old tellers are almost always people's favorites. There are good reasons for this. When people listened to the old tellers, they learned about God and about what God wanted them to do.

It is a sad thing to know, but many people who say they are tellers are faking it. They have not heard God. Everything they say is stuff they just made up. It is really bad to fool people into believing that you are a teller when you are just a faker.

When lots of years pass, the fake tellers and the real tellers are easy to tell apart. People keep listening to the real tellers year after year. The fake tellers just fade away when people realize that you can't learn anything about God by listening to what they have to tell. Sometimes a fake teller can fool people for a long time, but sooner or later, people will get tired of listening. And that is why people often trust the old tellers more than the new tellers. They have been around longer. What they have to tell has been checked out. What they have to tell is true.

How do you check out a teller? How do you know without waiting a long, long time if what a person is telling is from God, or just something that a fake teller made up? One way to check out tellers is to really listen to what the tellers are telling. Are they telling you to hurt somebody else? Are they telling you to run away from home? Are they telling you to do something that you always thought was bad? Are they telling you not ever to listen to any other tellers? Are they asking you to give them money before they will tell you anything? If a teller tells you to do any of these things, it is a very good bet that he or she is a fake teller and not a real teller.

Real tellers, the ones who really hear God and who really tell what God wants us to know, never ask you to hurt anyone else, or not to listen to other tellers, or to run away from home, or to give money before they tell you anything. They want only to bring you closer to God, and closer to each other. They want you to do what you know is good and right in your heart, and they want you to help people and live a good and clean life. What they tell is not news to you, but it sure is important.

Of course, the fact that people like old tellers more than new tellers makes it hard for a new teller to get heard. But if you are a real teller, you don't care how many people hear you. You just care that you tell exactly what God has told you.

Who can be a teller? The answer to this may surprise you. *Anyone can be a teller!* All of us are made special by God. All of us have ears to hear God. Even deaf people have ears to hear God, because God does not tell us things the way our Uncle Louie or Aunt Sarah tells us things. God speaks right to our souls. God makes us know right away just what we are supposed to know. So you don't need to be able to hear with your ears to hear God, and you don't need to be able to see with your eyes to see God. Anyone can be a teller.

Now, to be a teller, you have to be able to hear God, so that you will know what to tell. Some tellers have to be quiet and listen really hard to hear God. They need to sit still, and get still, and be quiet, and forget about anything but God. Then they can say, "Okay, God, I am ready to hear you and I am ready to be a teller to others of what you say to me."

Other tellers can hear God when they are doing other things. They hear God through the things they are doing. The things they are doing help them to feel God near them, and then they can say, "Okay, God, I am ready to hear you and I am ready to be a teller to others of what you say to me." Different tellers have different ways of hearing God and different ways of telling what they have heard. So you need to find your own best way of listening and telling.

Now, if you do all this, will God speak to you? Maybe yes, and maybe no. There is just no way to know for sure when God will speak to you, or what God will say. Good tellers seem to be able to listen better than most of us, so they hear better what God has to say. It is just like painting a picture. Everybody can paint something, but only a few really good painters can paint something really great. Why is that? We don't know why, it just is that way. God gives each of us special blessings, special gifts. One of the things we must do as we grow up is to discover what blessings God has given us. Some people are given the blessing of God to be really good tellers, and some are given the blessing to be really good listeners. Anyway, more people can be good tellers than can be good painters.

Maybe you will be the next great teller on planet earth. Maybe God will tell you something that we all need to know, and only you are given the message. So get ready, listen well, and for the sake of God, tell just what you are told.

17

WHAT DOES GOD WANT ME TO DO?

Telling is not enough. We must also do. God does not talk to us just for the fun of it. God talks to us to remind us what we should be doing to make the world a better, cleaner, safer, more wonderful place and to make us more loving of each other, and of God. If we think that once we tell about God, our job is done, we have to think again. God wants us to do good stuff, not just think good stuff or tell about good stuff.

Now, the way we see it, what God wants us to do is divided into different piles of boxes filled with things to do. There is one big pile of boxes of things to do which is the stuff God wants everybody to do. Near the big pile of boxes there are also many little piles of boxes, which is the stuff God wants just Jews to do or just Christians to do or just Muslims to do or just Hindus to do.

The first pile of boxes—for everybody—has things in it like helping poor people, and loving our parents, and not stealing, and not murdering, not hurting in any way. These are the kinds of things God wants all people to do, no matter who they are or where they live or what they believe. This is the stuff that, when we do it, makes the world better for everybody, and when we don't do it, it makes the world scary and awful.

God tells us all to do the things from the boxes in the big pile, but it's up to each of us to find out the ways we will do them. One box in the big pile tells us to love our neighbor the way we love ourselves, but God does not tell us just exactly how to do that. We have to find that out ourselves. God tells us to forgive, but not how to forgive. God tells us to make peace, but not how to work for peace. God tells us to feed the hungry, but not how to feed the hungry. God tells us to rest and not work all the time, but not how. God tells us what to do, but we have to figure out how to do it in our own special way.

We know a woman who works as a waitress to get money. Then she takes the money and uses it to buy medicine and stuff to heal birds who have been hurt. She fixes up the birds if she can, and feeds them, and protects them until they are better, and then she lets them go free. Fixing hurt birds is her special way of helping animals, which is one of the things in the big pile that God wants us all to do. That wonderful woman has found her own special way of doing something from the big pile.

We also know a woman who helps poor, sick people in the slums of India. She goes out every day and tries to do for people what the bird lady does for birds. Helping poor, sick people is her way of helping people, which is in the big pile of things God wants us all to do.

You, too, can find your own special way to do the things in the boxes in the big pile. You can watch people who do good things. You can help people who do good things. You can pray to God. The main thing is that you and only you can find your own special way to do the things in the boxes in the big pile. God will help you, but you have to do the looking, and you have to do the doing.

Remember that the big pile of boxes of things for everybody to do in our own special way is just one of the piles of things God wants us to do. There are also many different smaller piles of boxes near the big pile, and in each one of these little piles of boxes are special things for us to do which God has given to people in each religion to do.

If you are a Christian, you should walk over to the Christian pile of things God wants you to do and do as many of those things as you can. In the Christian pile are things that Christians are supposed to do and that are special and wonderful for Christians. Things like going to church, receiving Communion, saying your prayers, singing the hymns, reading the Bible, remembering and being happy at the birth of Jesus and decorating a tree at Christmas, remembering the death and life of Jesus and painting eggs on Easter, feeling especially close to God during Advent and Lent, and doing all the special Christian things and eating all the special foods of the holidays which are wonderful to do and to eat and which God has put in the Christian pile of things to do.

If you are a Jew, you should walk over to the Jewish pile of things God wants you to do and do as many of those things as you can. In the Jewish pile are things that Jews are supposed to do and that are special and wonderful for Jewish people to do. Things like going to the synagogue, saying the prayers and singing the hymns and reading the Bible, being happy at Rosh Hashana, not eating anything and praying all day on Yom Kippur, building a Sukkah, dancing with the Torah, lighting the Chanukah candles, dressing up in costumes and making noise on Purim, remembering the going out from Egypt and eating matzos on Passover, thanking God for giving the Torah on Shavuos and doing all the special Jewish things and eating all the special holiday foods which are wonderful to do and to eat and which God has put in the Jewish pile of things to do.

Every religion has its own pile of special and beautiful things to do which God wants each of us to do.

Now, you might want to know why God didn't just put down one big pile of boxes of things to do. You might ask, "Why did God make a whole bunch of piles of boxes of things to do?" Well, you have to know about singing to know the answer. When people sing a song and everybody sings the same notes, the song will probably be very boring, and will probably not be very beautiful. But when the singers each sing some different notes that blend together, the song is interesting and can be much more beautiful than if everybody just sang the same notes. And that is why God made a whole bunch of little piles of boxes near the big pile.

When each of us does the stuff in the big pile, the world is better, and more loving, and more peaceful, and there is less hurting and crying in the world. And when each of us does the stuff in the little piles, we are better inside and outside, and the world is filled with many different ways of singing our love for God. And that song is much more beautiful than it would be if we were all singing the same notes. By doing the things in the big pile we give the world love. By doing the things in the little piles we give harmony to the world and to ourselves and our lives. Harmony is when many people are singing together but they are not all singing the same notes.

So let us go out right now and start doing some more of the things God wants us to do. Let us try to help the whole world to sing with better harmony. We are God's hands and arms doing the stuff in the big pile and the stuff in the little piles which God needs done, and which we need done, and which the world needs done. But more than that, we are God's voices in the world.

We are the singers of God's song of love.

Here are some additional questions. They may help you to continue thinking and talking about God.

1. Where do you feel closest to God?
2. When did you last hear your inside voice?
3. What is your favorite part of the Bible?
4. What person do you know who has let God into his/her life the most?
5. What do you think God looks like?
6. What was the last little miracle you saw?
7. Who will you want to see when you get to heaven or the world to come?
8. What was the last really good thing you chose to do?
9. What is the one bad thing in the world you would like to change?
10. How have you helped somebody who was in pain?
11. If your good deeds were all piled on one side of a scale and your bad deeds on the other side, which way would the scales tip?
12. What are you most angry at God about?
13. What do you say to God in most of your prayers?
14. Who do you love?
15. If you had to explain your religion to somebody else, what would you say?
16. Who is your favorite teller?
17. What do you want to do for God in your life?

MY FRIEND TOM HARTMAN

Tom is a priest who loves people, appears on television, and spends a lot of time praying and helping people. He runs a television station on Long Island which shows religious programs. Tom is on television a lot and he is very good at asking questions and very, very good at listening to the answers. Tom also loves music and has a radio show on which he plays rock and roll music and talks about what the songs mean. Tom thinks that some rock and roll songs are like poems, and I think he is right. Tom works very hard. He always gets up before I get up and he always goes to sleep after I go to sleep. Many people who are sad or angry come to Tom because he is so very kind. Tom can make anybody feel better just by being with them. He lives on Long Island, and teaches many children. Tom is one of my very best friends.

Rabbi Marc Gellman

MY FRIEND MARC GELLMAN

Marc is a rabbi who loves people, appears on television, and spends a lot of time praying and helping people. He is the rabbi of a synagogue called Temple Beth Torah on Long Island. He is married to Betty, who is a kind and wonderful woman. Marc and Betty have two children: Mara, who is off at college in Colorado, and Max, who is still in high school. Mara is a great painter. Max is tall and plays the sax and first base. They have a little white dog named Willie, and a bunch of fish. Marc is a great writer and teller of stories. His first book was called *Does God Have a Big Toe? Stories About Stories in the Bible*. I love the stories in that book. Marc is also a doctor—a doctor of philosophy, which means he knows a lot, but he can't take

out your appendix. Marc has taught in college
and in many places where people have learned
from him. Marc is one of my very best friends.

Thomas Hartman

Monsignor Thomas Hartman

About the Authors

Rabbi Marc Gellman is the rabbi of Temple Beth Torah in Melville, NY, holds a doctorate in philosophy, and has taught philosophy, theology, medical ethics, and creative writing. He is author of the award-winning children's book *Does God Have a Big Toe?*.

Monsignor Thomas Hartman, D.Min., serves at the Rockville Centre Diocese in Rockville Centre, NY, where he has won two Emmy Awards as Director of Radio and Television and hosts a national radio program, "Journeys Through Rock."

They have a weekly national TV program, "The God Squad," which reaches sixteen million homes. They appear frequently on national TV programs and have won much praise for their dogma-free approach to religion.